SoPHIE LEARNS
SPANISH

Illustrated by Annabel Tempest
Written by Sue Finnie & Libby Mitchell

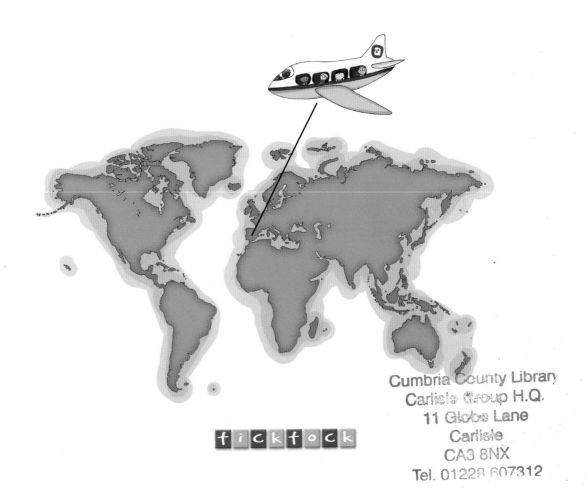

ticktock

Copyright © ticktock Entertainment Ltd 2007
First published in Great Britain in 2007 by ticktock Media Ltd.,
Unit 2, Orchard Business Centre, North Farm Road,
Tunbridge Wells, Kent, TN2 3XF

ticktock project editor: Ruth Owen
ticktock project designer: Emma Randall

Text by Sue Finnie and Libby Mitchell
Illustrations by Annabel Tempest

ISBN-13: 978 1 84696 652 1 pbk

Printed in China

¡Hola!

Welcome to Spain. Join our visit to this amazing country, and learn the basics of the Spanish language along the way.

1 Read

Follow Sophie and Pablo's adventures in Spain as they take part in a fiesta, watch a football match and much more.

2 Learn

All the Spanish words in this book are in **bold.** If you want to find out what they mean, turn to the handy phrasebook on pages 30 and 31. There is also an easy-to-follow guide to pronunciation to help you speak Spanish.

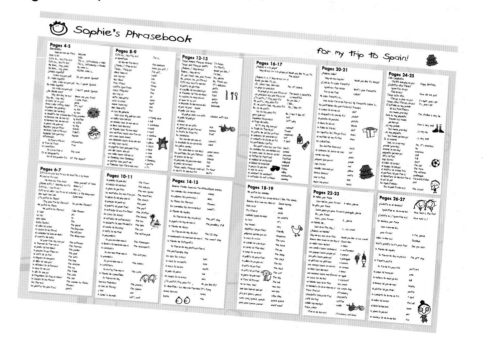

Sophie's Phrasebook — for my trip to Spain!

After a very long plane ride, Sophie has finally arrived in Spain. She is going to stay for a week with her friend Pablo and his family. She's never met them before. How will she get along?

LLEGADAS

SERVICIOS

EQUIPAJE

INFORMACIÓN

Este es mi hermano. Se llama Juan.

Esta es mi abuelita. Se llama María.

Este es mi padre. Se llama Manuel.

Hola. Me llamo Sophie.

Esta es mi madre. Se llama Violeta.

Hola. Me llamo Pablo.

Este es mi perro. Se llama Curro.

Pablo says hello: **"¡Hola! Me llamo Pablo."** He asks if Sophie speaks Spanish. **"¿Hablas español?" "Sí, hablo español"** she replies. Luckily, she speaks a bit of Spanish and she has her little phrasebook. (It will be useful for you too!)

4

Outside the airport, Sophie points at the sun. **"¡Hace calor!"** Yes, it is hot. Sophie and Pablo both like hot weather. But it's TOO hot for Curro with his warm coat. Poor Curro!

Say your name in Spanish.

Me llamo...

la carretera

el taxi

"¿De dónde eres?" The taxi driver is asking Sophie where she comes from. **"Soy de London"** she smiles.

"Esta es mi casa." This is Pablo's house. Curro finds a great way to cool down while Pablo welcomes Sophie to his home: **"Mi casa es tu casa."** He's telling her to make herself at home.

la lámpara

el salón

el sofá

el sillón

la alfombra

la piscina

In the garden and on the terrace, there are lots of colourful plants and flowers. Pablo asks Sophie if she likes flowers: *"¿Te gustan las flores?"* Sophie nods yes: *"¡Sí!"* She loves flowers: *"¡Me gustan las flores!"*

Where is Curro the dog?

Está en...

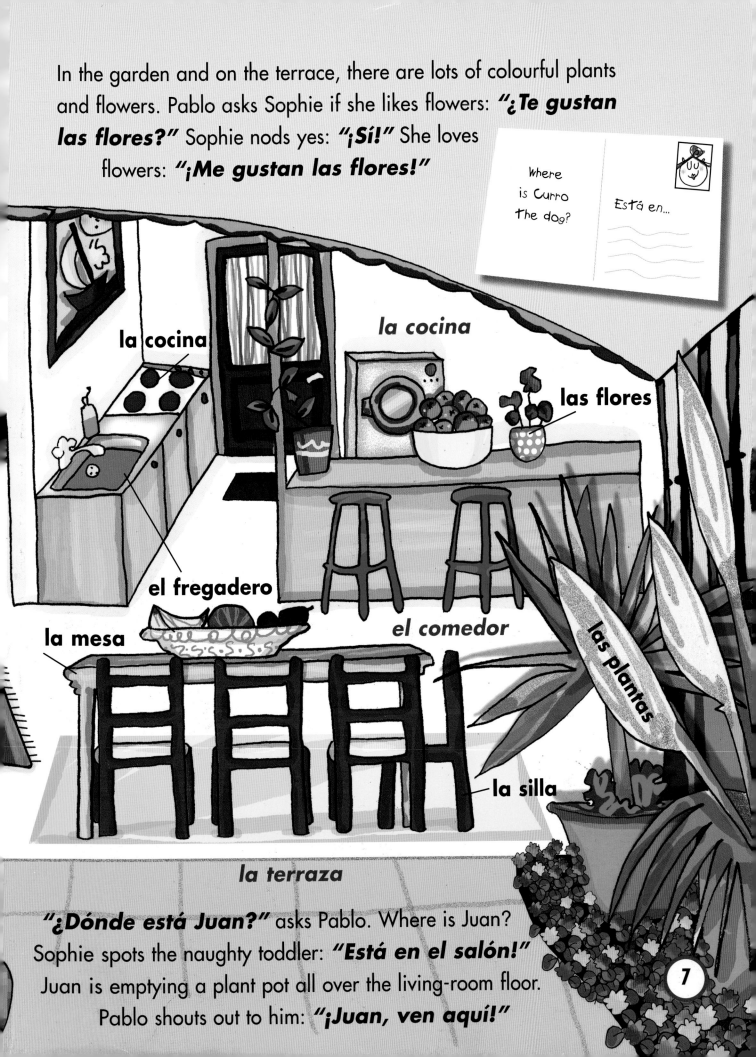

la cocina

la cocina

las flores

el fregadero

la mesa

el comedor

las plantas

la silla

la terraza

"¿Dónde está Juan?" asks Pablo. Where is Juan?
Sophie spots the naughty toddler: *"Está en el salón!"*
Juan is emptying a plant pot all over the living-room floor.
Pablo shouts out to him: *"¡Juan, ven aquí!"*

Este es el dormitorio. Pablo's bedroom is full of really interesting things. He's a big football fan and very proud of his collection of football shirts. Sophie counts them with him: *"Uno, dos, tres, cuatro, cinco, seis, siete, ocho, nueve, diez."*

un oso de peluche

un balón

una ventana

un tejado

un armario

uno

dos

un libro

seis

tres

cuatro

cinco

siete

ocho

nueve

Ten football shirts! Juan has a look in the wardrobe, just to check if there are any more. But he can't find any and shakes his head: *"¡No!"*

Pablo has lots of things in his room. He explains: **"Tengo un balón, un póster, una radio..."** Sophie looks around to see if there is a TV. She asks: **"¿Tienes un televisor?"** but Pablo doesn't have a TV set in his bedroom.

Say what you've got in your room.

Tengo...

un póster

una almohada

un pupitre

un reloj

diez

un Gameboy

una cama

una silla

una radio

Then Sophie spots something strange... an enormous pillow! She tells Pablo to look: **"¡Mira!"** Pablo laughs: it's just Curro playing hide-and-seek under the pillow.

Where in the town would you go to...
a) see a boat?
b) catch a train?
c) see a film?

You can see lots of places from the balcony. Pablo points out some places to Sophie: *"Mira, Sophie. El puerto, la iglesia, la plaza y las casas."* Little Juan can see mountains in the distance. *"¡Las montañas, las montañas!"* he calls.

las montañas

el parque

la pescadería

el autobús

el tren

la librería

la carnicería

la panadería

la bicicleta

el balcón

la moto

la plaza

10

Sophie is looking forward to exploring the town with Pablo, but she is very hungry. She is glad when her aunt calls: *"¡A comer!"* It must be lunchtime!

la estación las casas

la iglesia

el puerto

la cafetería

la tienda de comestibles

el cine

el coche

"Tengo hambre." Sophie is really hungry as it's much later than she usually eats. Her aunt offers her some chicken with rice: **"¿Quieres pollo con arroz, Sophie?"** Sophie nods: **"¡Sí, por favor!"** She tells them all it's delicious: **"¡Está rico!"** Now Sophie is thirsty. **"Tengo sed."** Pablo offers her some lemonade. **"¿Quieres limonada?"** Yes please! she replies. **"¡Sí, por favor!"**

el plato

el pan
el pollo
las zanahorias

el jamón
el tenedor

la limonada
las judías verdes
la ensalada
el cuchillo

el queso
el pescado
el arroz
la cuchara

los pasteles

el plátano

When her aunt offers her more, Sophie is so full she has to say no: **"¡No, gracias!"** Juan wants another banana though: **"¡Quiero un plátano!"** Everybody starts laughing.

After lunch, Grandma yawns and says she's tired: **"Tengo sueño."** It's siesta time and everyone has a rest or a nap, including the dog. Pablo explains that they often stay indoors and rest for a while after lunch as it's too hot to go outside.

Say what you want to eat or drink.

Quiero...

Sophie thinks it's unusual, but she soon nods off after her long journey and her huge lunch, even though Grandma and Curro are both snoring like growling lions!

Later on it's the evening paseo. Everyone comes out to walk about and meet and chat with their friends. Her aunt and uncle greet everybody they know, saying: **"¡Buenas tardes!"**

LA TIENDA DE REGALOS

la joyería

LA TIENDA DE DISCOS

los caramelos

las flores

los animales

los pájaros

Sophie is fascinated by all the stalls and street entertainers. She wants to buy a songbird but her aunt persuades her to buy sweets – **caramelos** – instead.

Juan starts to cry when his balloon flies away into the night sky. He cheers up a bit when he sees Curro trying to help the juggler. Everyone shouts: **"¡Bravo!"** – what a clever dog!

Point to the different parts of your face and say what they are called in Spanish.

la bombonería

LA TIENDA DE FOTOGRAFÍA

el pelo   los ojos
la nariz
las orejas
la boca

An artist draws a cartoon picture of Sophie and asks her if she likes it: **"¿Te gusta?"** Sophie thinks it's funny: **"Es divertido!"**

15

The following morning Pablo asks Sophie if she would like to go to the beach: *"¿Quieres ir a la playa?"* *"¡Sí, claro!"* replies Sophie with delight. She loves the beach!

la pesca

la vela

la natación

el windsurf

el sombrero

las gafas de sol

la camiseta

la toalla

los pantalones cortos

16

las sandalias

el traje de baño

The sand is white and the sea is clear and turquoise blue. It's the most beautiful beach Sophie has ever seen. **"La playa es preciosa,"** she says to Pablo. **"¡Juguemos!"** Pablo is delighted to have a friend to play with on the beach. **"¿Te gusta el fútbol? ¿Te gusta el béisbol?"** he asks Sophie. **"Sí, me gusta el fútbol y me gusta el béisbol...pero no me gusta la pesca."** She likes football and baseball but she doesn't like fishing.

el voleibol

el béisbol

el fútbol

la crema solar

Look at the beach and say what you like doing.

Me gusta...

The next day, Pablo takes Sophie to meet the animals at Tío Antonio´s ranch. *"Buenos días, Tío Antonio,"* Pablo calls to his uncle. *"¡Hola, Pablo! ¡Hola, Sophie!"* he replies, smiling. Pablo can imitate the animals´ noises. *"Mu mu, bee bee, cuac cuac, pío pío."* Sophie laughs so much that Curro starts barking: *"¡Guau, guau, guau!"*

la oveja

el caballo

la vaca

el perro

el toro

Cuidado!

el cerdo

Pablo says **"Cuidado, Sophie. El toro es peligroso."** But Sophie isn't worried about the fierce bull. **"Me gusta el pollito."** She likes the chick. **"Es muy simpático."** It's very friendly.

el gato

el pato

la gallina

Say which animals you like.

Me gusta...

el pollito

Today is an important day – there is a fiesta in the town. Sophie and Pablo are wearing special clothes. There are games and singing and dancing. Pablo asks Sophie to dance: *"¿Quieres bailar?"*

púrpura

verde

amarillo

rojo

la chaqueta

los pantalones

los calcetines

el vestido

los zapatos

There are even fireworks to watch. *"¿Cuál es tu color favorito?"* asks Pablo. *"Mi color favorito es azul"* says Sophie. She likes blue best. Pablo prefers the red firework. *"Mi color favorito es el rojo."*

blanco

azul

What's your favourite colour?

Mi color favorito es

el poncho

el sombrero

la camisa

la falda

la blusa

21

una piña

un plátano

una manzana

una naranja

una sandía

un limón

una papaya

un melón

un coco

Pablo and Sophie are buying some fruit at the market. Sophie loves the colours of all the different fruit. The pineapples and oranges look delicious and very juicy. The papayas are huge! But in the end Sophie asks for a melon. **"Un melón, por favor."** Pablo wants a pineapple: **"Una piña, por favor."**

"¿Quieres un helado, Sophie?" asks Pablo, pointing at the ice cream shop. Sophie says that's a good idea: **"¡Buena idea!"** She can remember some of the names of the fruit to help her choose her ice cream: **"Un helado de fresa, limón y mango, por favor."** Pablo looks at the other flavours on the ice cream board and asks for **"Chocolate, vainilla y fresa."**

Ask for the ice cream you would like.

Un helado de...

La de Micho

piña
limón
naranja
coco
fresa
chocolate
café
vainilla

un helado

23

On Friday there's a big football match in the stadium. It's Pablo's birthday, and for a special treat the family are going to see the big game. *"¡Feliz cumpleaños!"* says Sophie. *"¿Cuántos años tienes?"* She's asking how old he is. *"Tengo ocho años."* Pablo is eight years old!

los espectadores

EL GOL

FÚTBOL F

el equipo

el portero

¡El gol!

Sophie is amazed at the size of the stadium. **"El estadio es muy grande,"** she says. **"Sí, es enorme,"** replies Pablo. Then Sophie looks at Juan. He's so little! **"Juan es muy pequeño,"** she says, laughing!

los espectadores

TBOL

el árbitro

el balón

el delantero

What is grande and who is pequeño?

La tienda de regalos

el juego

el póster

el abanico

la camiseta

la tarjeta postal

el balón

el llavero

la pluma

el libro

la muñeca

It's the last day of Sophie's holiday. She wants to buy some presents to take home. She chooses dolls for her Mum and Dad, and something for Pablo and Juan too. As she has a little bit of money left, Sophie wants to know how much the fan is.

(26) *"¿Cuánto es el abanico?"* she asks. It costs six euros. She decides to buy one. *"Un abanico, por favor,"* Sophie asks the shopkeeper.

Sophie says goodbye to everyone.
"Adiós, Pablo. Adiós, Juan. Adiós, Curro."
They are all so sad to see her go but they hope she'll
come back soon. **"Adiós, Sophie. ¡Hasta pronto!"**

"Adiós, Pablo. Adiós, Juan. Adiós, Curro!"

My Spanish Holiday Scrapbook

Pablo lives here

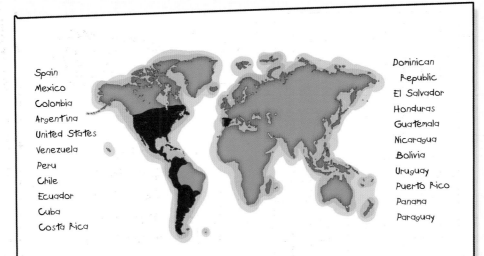

Spain
Mexico
Colombia
Argentina
United States
Venezuela
Peru
Chile
Ecuador
Cuba
Costa Rica

Dominican Republic
El Salvador
Honduras
Guatemala
Nicaragua
Bolivia
Uruguay
Puerto Rico
Panama
Paraguay

The shaded areas on the map show where Spanish is spoken in the world.

Spain is famous for its fiestas, celebrations of music and dancing.

DOMINGO	Arrive at Pablo's home. Have a look round. Evening: paseo.
LUNES	A day on the beach. Terrific!
MARTES	Tío Antonio's ranch. The animals are cool.
MIÉRCOLES	Fiesta.
JUEVES	Buying fruit at the market and eating ice creams.
VIERNES	¡El partido! The football match.
SÁBADO	Time to go home! I hope I can come back to see Pablo next year!

Enero										
Febrero										
Marzo										
Abril										
Mayo										
Junio										
Julio										
Agosto										
Septiembre										
Octubre										
Noviembre										
Diciembre										

Pablo has helped Sophie make a Spanish year planner. Why don't you use it too?

You too could make a scrapbook next holiday!

Sophie's Phrasebook

Pages 4-5

Bienvenidos (bee-en-ven-ee-thos) — Welcome
Hola (o-la) — Hello
Este es... (ess-tay ess) — This is... (introducing a male)
Esta es... (ess-ta ess) — This is... (introducing a female)
Me llamo... (may yamo) — My name is...
Se llama... (say yama) — His/Her name is...
¿Hablas español? (a-blas ess-pan-yol?) — Do you speak Spanish?
Sí, hablo español (see, a-blo ess-pan-yol) — Yes, I speak Spanish
No hablo español (no a-blo ess-pan-yol) — I don't speak Spanish
¿De dónde eres? (day don-day air-ess) — Where are you from?
Soy de... (soy day) — I come from...
el avión (el av-yon) — plane
Hace calor (athay kalor) — It's hot
mi padre (me pardray) — my dad
mi madre (me madray) — my mom
mi abuelita (me a-bwee-lee-ta) — my grandma
mi hermano (me air-mar-no) — my brother
mi hermana (me air-mar-na) — my sister
mi perro (me pair-ro) — my dog
llegadas (yay-ga-thas) — arrivals
servicios (sair-vi-thi-uss) — toilets
equipaje (ek-i-par-hay) — luggage
información (in-form-a-thi-on) — information
el taxi (el taxi) — taxi
la carretera (la ca-re-tair-a) — the road
En el aeropuerto (en el ero-pwehr-to) — At the airport

Pages 6-7

Esta es mi casa (ess-ta ess me kasa) — This is my house
Mi casa es tu casa (me kasa ess too kasa) — Make yourself at home
¿Dónde está...? (don-day ess-ta) — Where is...?
Está en... (ess-ta en) — He's in...
Está en el salón (ess-ta en el sa-lon) — He's in the living-room
¡Ven aquí! (ven aki) — Come here!
¿Te gustan las flores? (tay goos-tan las flor-ess?) — Do you like flowers?
Me gustan las flores (me gustan las flor-ess) — I like flowers
sí (see) — Yes
no (no) — No
el/la (el/la) — the
los/las (los/las) — the (plural)
el salón (el sa-lon) — the living-room
la cocina (la ko-thi-na) — the kitchen
el comedor (el kom-air-dohr) — the dining-room
el cuarto de baño (el quar-toe day ban-yo) — the bathroom
la terraza (la tair-raz-a) — the terrace
el jardín (el har-deen) — the garden
la piscina (la pis-thee-na) — the pool
el sofá (el so-fah) — the sofa
la lámpara (la lam-para) — the lamp
el sillón (el see-yon) — the armchair
la alfombra (la al-fom-bra) — the rug
la mesa (la me-ssa) — the table
la silla (la see-ya) — the chair
el fregadero (el freg-ar-dairo) — the sink
la cocina (la ko-thi-na) — the cooker
las flores (las flor-ess) — flowers
las plantas (las plan-tass) — plants

Pages 8-9

Este es... (ess-tay ess) — This is...
el dormitorio (el dor-me-tor-ee-o) — the bedroom
¿Tienes...? (tee-en-es) — Have you got...?
Tengo... (teng-o) — I've got...
¡Mira! (mee-ra) — Look!
uno (oo-no) — one
dos (doss) — two
tres (tress) — three
cuatro (qua-troe) — four
cinco (thing-ko) — five
seis (say-ss) — six
siete (see-yete) — seven
ocho (o-choe) — eight
nueve (nwe-vay) — nine
diez (dee-eth) — ten

un oso de peluche (oon osso day pell-oo-che) — a teddy bear
un balón (oon bal-on) — a ball
un armario (oon ar-mar-ee-o) — a wardrobe
un libro (oon lee-bro) — a book
un tejado (oon te-har-doe) — a roof
una ventana (oona ven-tar-na) — a window
una cama (oona kama) — a bed
una almohada (oona al-mo-ahr-da) — a pillow
un reloj (oon ray-lo) — a clock
un pupitre (oon poo-pee-tray) — a desk
una silla (oona see-ya) — a chair
una radio (oona rad-ee-o) — a radio
un Gameboy (oon Gameboy) — a Gameboy
un póster (oon post-air) — a poster
un televisor (oon tel-e-vee-saw) — a tv

Pages 10-11

el pueblo (el pue-blo) — the town
el balcón (el bal-kon) — the balcony
la plaza (la pla-tha) — the main square
las montañas (las mon-tan-yas) — the mountains
la iglesia (la ee-glay-see-a) — the church
el parque (el park-ay) — the park
el puerto (el pwer-toe) — the port
la estación (la ess-ta-thion) — the station
las casas (las kasas) — the houses
el autobús (el outoe-boos) — the bus
la bicicleta (la bee-thi-kleta) — The bike
el coche (el ko-chay) — The car
la moto (la mo-toe) — The motorcycle
la pescadería (la pess-ka-dair-ree-a) — the fishmongers
la librería (la lee-brair-ree-a) — The newsagents
la carnicería (la kar-nee-thair-ree-a) — The butchers
la panadería (la pa-na-dair-ree-a) — the bakers
la cafetería (la ka-fay-tair-ree-a) — the cafe
la tienda de comestibles (la tee-en-da day kom-ess-teeb-less) — The grocers
el cine (el thi-nay) — the cinema
y (ee) — and
A comer (a ko-main) — Let's eat

Pages 12-13

Tengo hambre (teng-go am-bray) — I'm hungry
Tengo sed (teng-go sedth) — I'm thirsty
¿Quieres...? (key-air-ess) — Would you like...?
Quiero... (key-air-o) — I'd like...
Sí, por favor (see, paw fa-vor) — Yes, please
No, gracias (no, gra-thi-ass) — No, thank you
Está rico (ess-ta ree-ko) — It's delicious
el plato (el pla-toe) — plate
el cuchillo (el ku-chee-ll-yo) — knife
el tenedor (el ten-air-door) — fork
la cuchara (la koo-cha-ra) — spoon
el agua (el ag-wa) — water
la limonada (la lee-mon-ar-da) — lemonade
el pan (el pan) — bread
el pollo con arroz (el poll-yo kohn a-rr-oth) — chicken with rice
el pollo (el poll-yo) — chicken
el arroz (el arr-oth) — rice
el plátano (el pla-tan-no) — banana
la fruta (la froo-ta) — fruit
las zanahorias (las zan-ahr-ohr-ree-as) — carrots
la ensalada (la en-sal-ad-da) — salad
las judías verdes (las who-dee-as vair-dess) — green beans
los pasteles (los pas-tell-ess) — cakes
el queso (el ke-so) — cheese
el pescado (el pess-kar-doe) — fish
el jamón (el ha-mon) — ham
Tengo sueño (teng-go swen-yo) — I'm tired
la siesta (la see-ess-ta) — siesta

Pages 14-15

Buenas tardes (bwe-nas tar-dthess) — Good evening
los animales (los an-ee-mal-ess) — animals
los pájaros (los pa-ha-ross) — birds
las flores (las flor-ess) — flowers
los caramelos (los ka-ra-me-loss) — sweets
la tienda de regalos (la tee-en-da day re-gal-oss) — the gift shop
la joyería (la hoy-air-ree-a) — the jewellery stall
la tienda de discos (la tee-en-da day dis-kos) — The CD shop
la bombonería (la bom-bon-air-ree-a) — The sweet shop
la tienda de fotografía (la tee-en-da day photo-gra-fee-a) — The photography shop
los ojos (los o-hoss) — eyes
la nariz (la na-reeth) — nose
la boca (la bo-ka) — mouth
el pelo (el pel-o) — hair
las orejas (la or-e-has) — ears
¿Te gusta? (tay goos-ta) — Do you like (it)?
Es divertido (ess dee-vair-tee-doe) — It's funny
bravo (bra-vo) — bravo
los/las — the (plural)

for my trip to Spain!

Pages 16-17

¿Quieres ir a la playa?
(key-air-ess i-rr a la pl-eye-ya) — Would you like to go to the beach?

¿Quieres ir a...? (key-air-ess i-rr a) — Would you like to go...

¡Sí, claro! (see, klar-roe) — Yes, of course.

La playa es preciosa
(la pl-eye-ya ess pre-thi-os-sa) — The beach is beautiful

...es preciosa (ess pre-thi-os-sa) — ...is beautiful

¿Te gusta...? (tay goos-ta) — Do you like...?

Me gusta... (may goos-ta) — I like...

Sí, me gusta (see, may goos-ta) — Yes, I like (it)

No, no me gusta (no no may goos-ta) — No, I don't like (it)

pero (pair-o) — but

Juguemos (hu-ga-moss) — Let's play

el traje de baño
(el tr-hay day ban-yo) — swimsuit

la toalla (la toe-al-ya) — towel

las gafas de sol (las ga-fass) — sunglasses

el sombrero (el som-brair-ro) — hat

la camiseta (la ka-me-se-ta) — t-shirt

los pantalones cortos
(los pant-a-lon-ess cor-tos) — shorts

las sandalias (las san-dal-lee-ass) — sandals

la crema solar (la kre-ma so-lar) — suncream

el fútbol (el foot-bol) — football

el voleibol (el vo-lay-bol) — volleyball

el béisbol (el base-bol) — baseball

la pesca (la pes-ka) — fishing

la vela (la ve-la) — sailing

el windsurf (el windsurf) — windsurfing

la natación (la nat-a-thion) — swimming

Pages 18-19

Me gustan los animales
(me goostan los an-ee-mal-ess) — I like the animals

Buenos días (we-nos dee-as) — Good morning

Hola (o-la) — Hello

tío (tee-o) — uncle

cuidado (quee-da-doe) — be careful

es (ess) — it's

muy (mwee) — very

simpático (sim-pa-tiko) — friendly

peligroso (pe-lee-gro-so) — dangerous

la vaca (la va-ka) — the cow

el caballo (el cab-al-yo) — the horse

el cerdo (el ther-doe) — the pig

la oveja (la ov-e-ha) — the sheep

el pollito (el pol-yi-toe) — the chick

la gallina (la ga-yee-na) — the hen

el pato (el pa-toe) — the duck

el gato (el ga-toe) — the cat

el perro (el pair-roe) — the dog

el toro (el to-roe) — the bull

mu mu (moo, moo) — moo moo

bee bee (beh-eh beh-eh) — baa baa

pío pío (pee-o, pee-o) — chirp chirp

cuac cuac (quack, quack) — quack quack

guau guau (gwow gwow) — woof woof

Pages 20-21

¿Quieres bailar?
(key-air-ress buy-lar) — Would you like to dance?

¿Cuál es tu color favorito?
(quarl ess too ko-lor fav-or-ee-toe) — What's your favourite colour?

Mi color favorito es...
(mee ko-lor fav-or-ee-toe ess) — My favourite colour is...

los pantalones (los pan-ta-lon-es) — trousers

la camisa (la ka-me-sa) — shirt

la chaqueta (la cha-ke-ta) — jacket

el poncho (el poncho) — poncho

la blusa (la blu-sa) — blouse

la falda (la fal-da) — skirt

los zapatos (los tha-pa-toss) — shoes

el vestido (el ves-ti-tho) — dress

los calcetines
(los kal-the-teen-ess) — socks

el sombrero (el som-br-air-oe) — hat

verde (ver-day) — green

púrpura (pur-pu-ra) — purple

rojo (ro-ho) — red

amarillo (ama-reel-yo) — yellow

blanco (blanco) — white

azul (a-thul) — blue

negro (ne-grow) — black

Pages 22-23

Un melón, por favor
(oon mel-on, paw fa-vor) — A melon, please

Un piña, por favor
(oona peen-ya, paw fa-vor) — A pineapple, please

Un... por favor
(oon... paw fa-vor) — A... please

un helado de...
(oon el-ar-tho day...) — a... ice cream

¿Quieres un helado?
(key-air-ess oon el-ar-tho) — Would you like an ice cream?

Buena idea (bwe-na ee-day-a) — Good idea

un melón (oon me-lon) — a melon

una sandía (oona sand-ee-a) — a watermelon

una papaya (oona pa-pie-ya) — a papaya

una piña (oona peen-ya) — a pineapple

un plátano (un plátano) — a banana

una naranja (oona na-ran-ha) — an orange

un limón (oon lee-mon) — a lemon

una manzana (oona man-tha-na) — an apple

un coco (on ko-ko) — a coconut

un helado (oon el-ar-tho) — ice cream

la heladería (la el-ar-dair-ee-a) — ice cream shop

fresa (frai-sa) — strawberry

chocolate (choco-lar-tay) — chocolate

café (ka-fay) — coffee

vainilla (viy-nee-llya) — vanilla

fresa y limón
(frai-sa ee lee-mon) — strawberry and lemon

Pages 24-25

Feliz cumpleaños
(fe-lith kum-play-an-yos) — Happy Birthday

¿Cuántos años tienes?
(quan-tos an-yos tee-en-ess) — How old are you?

Tengo ocho años
(ten-go o-choe an-yos) — I'm eight years old

Tengo...años (ten-go...an-yos) — I'm... years old

El estadio es muy grande
(el ess-tard-thee-o ess mwee gran-day) — The stadium is very big

Juan es muy pequeño
(hwuarn ess mwee pe-ken-yo) — Juan is very small

...es muy grande
(ess mwee gran-day) — ...is very big

...es muy pequeño
(ess mwee pe-ken-yo) — ...is very small

Sí, es enorme
(see, es e-nor-may) — Yes, it's enormous

grande (gran-day) — big

enorme (e-nor-may) — enormous

pequeño (pe-ken-yo) — small

alto (al-toe) — tall

bajo (ba-ho) — short

el balón (el ba-lon) — the ball

el equipo (el eki-po) — the team

el árbitro (el ar-bee-tro) — the referee

el portero (el por-tair-o) — goalkeeper

el delantero (el dea-lan-tair-o) — forward/striker

el gol (el gol) — goal

los espectadores
(los es-pek-ta-dor-ess) — the crowd

Pages 26-27

¿Cuánto es el abanico?
(quan-toe es ab-an-ee-ko) — How much is the fan?

¿Cuánto es...? (quan-toe ess) — How much is...?

Un abanico, por favor
(oon a-ban-ee-ko, paw fa-vor) — A fan, please

Adiós (a-dee-oss) — Goodbye

Hasta pronto (as-ta pron-toe) — See you soon

la tienda de regalas
(la tee-en-da day re-gal-oss) — the gift shop

la tarjeta postal
(la tar-he-ta poss-tal) — postcard

el juego (el hway-go) — game

la muñeca (la moon-ye-ka) — doll

el llavero (el yav-air-roe) — keyring

el póster (el po-stair) — poster

la camiseta (la ka-me-se-ta) — t-shirt

el balón (el ba-lon) — the ball

el libro (el lee-bro) — book

la pluma (la plu-ma) — pen

el abanico (el ab-an-ee-ko) — fan

Matching pictures and words

1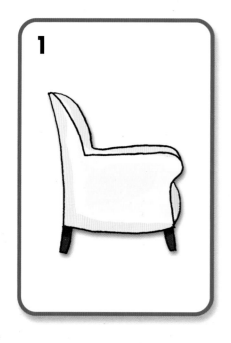

2

3

el plátano

la muñeca

la camiseta

el autobús

el pato

el sillón

4

5

6

1 el sillón 2 el autobús 3 el pato 4 el plátano 5 la muñeca 6 la camiseta